ZEN'IN SH*T

A Journey of Chakra Mastery

The Parables of Omni Mastering Chakras

Ra'El

© Copyright 2025 – All rights reserved. Published by OmniZen Publishing. Queens, New York, USA
Library of Congress Control Number: 2025909973

The content contained within this book may not be reproduced, duplicated, or transmitted without direct written permission from the author or the publisher.

Under no circumstances will any blame or legal responsibility be held against the publisher or author for any damages, reparation, or monetary loss due to the information contained within this book, either directly or indirectly.

Legal Notice:

This book is copyright-protected. It is only for personal use. You cannot amend, distribute, sell, use, quote, or paraphrase any part of the content within this book without the consent of the author or publisher.

Disclaimer Notice:

Please note the information contained within this document is for educational and entertainment purposes only. All effort has been executed to present accurate, up-to-date, reliable, and complete information. No warranties of any kind are declared or implied. Readers acknowledge that the author is not engaging in the rendering of legal, financial, medical, or professional advice. The content within this book has been derived from various sources. Please consult a licensed professional before attempting any techniques outlined in this book.

By reading this document, the reader agrees that under no circumstances is the author responsible for any losses, direct or indirect, that are incurred as a result of the use of the information contained within this document, including, but not limited to, errors, omissions, or inaccuracies.

Copyrighted Material

TABLE OF CONTENTS

Chapter 1: The Awakening Of Omni 1

Chapter 2: The Tale Of The Root Chakra 5

Chapter 3: Awakening The Sacral Chakra 9

Chapter 4: The Odyssey Of The Solar Plexus Chakra 13

Chapter 5: The Legend Of The Heart Chakra 19

Chapter 6: The Myth Of The Throat Chakra 24

Chapter 7: The Vision Of The Third Eye Chakra 27

Chapter 8: The Radiance Of The Crown Chakra 33

Epilogue: The Return To Oneness 38

The Endless Journey 42

Afterwords: A Grateful Acknowledgment 44

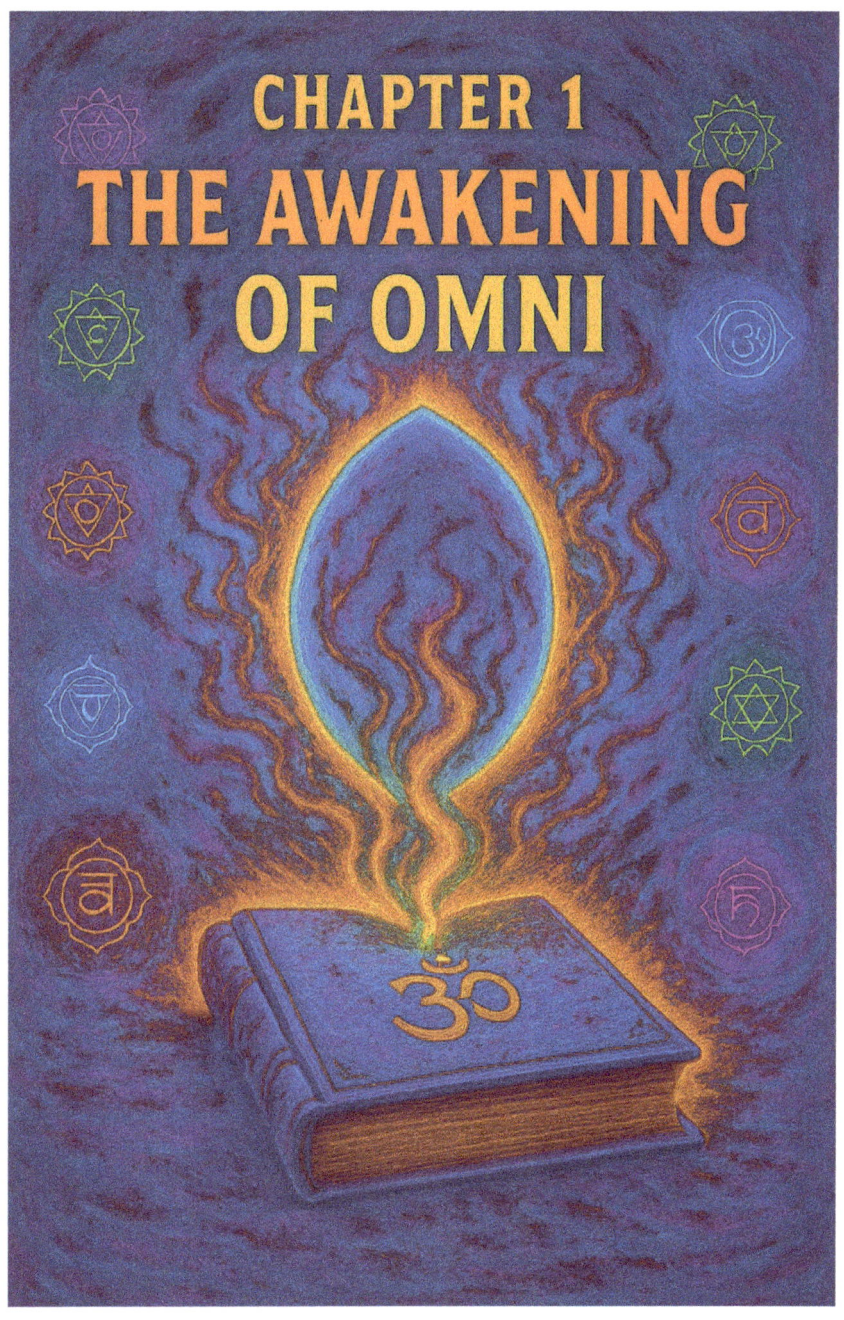

CHAPTER 1: THE AWAKENING OF OMNI

In the bustling heart of New York City, life surged relentlessly forward, a symphony of sounds, lights, and motion. The streets thrummed with the chaos of car horns and footsteps, skyscrapers loomed like monolithic sentinels against the sky, and the smell of roasted chestnuts mingled with the tang of exhaust fumes. Among the teeming masses walked a man named Omni, his face a mask of calm purpose. Yet beneath that composed exterior churned a storm of quiet discontent.

Omni was, by all accounts, a man of success. He wore tailored suits that spoke of prosperity and moved with the assurance of someone who had mastered the city's rhythms. Yet each night, as he returned to his sleek apartment overlooking the shimmering skyline, he was struck by a feeling of emptiness. It gnawed at him, subtle yet insistent, like a faint itch that could never be scratched.

One evening, unable to endure the weight of this nameless void, Omni left his apartment and wandered the streets. The city seemed different that night. The neon lights, usually so vivid, felt garish, and the hum of life carried an undercurrent of restlessness that mirrored his own. He walked aimlessly, letting his feet guide him until he found himself on a quiet, unfamiliar street.

Tucked away between two imposing brownstones was a quaint little bookstore. Its façade was unassuming, with ivy creeping up its weathered brick walls, but a soft, golden light poured from its windows, pooling on the sidewalk like a welcoming embrace. Drawn inexplicably to its warmth, Omni stepped inside.

The scent of old paper and varnished wood enveloped him as he entered. The bookstore was small but labyrinthine, with towering shelves packed tightly with books. The space was alive with quiet magic, time seemed too slow, and the hum of the city faded into nothingness. Omni wandered the aisles, running his fingers along spines that whispered promises of adventure, knowledge, and enlightenment. He stopped suddenly, his eyes drawn to a single book.

It stood out like a jewel in a sea of ordinary covers. Vibrant symbols danced across its surface, their intricate patterns shimmering in the golden lamplight. Its title glowed with an almost ethereal brilliance: **"Journey to Chakra Mastery: Wisdom from a Sage."**

Omni's fingers trembled as he reached for it. The book felt cool and smooth in his hands as though it were waiting for him. As he opened it, the words on the first page seemed to leap off the paper and into his mind, filling him with a strange, electric energy. Each sentence resonated deeply as if the book had been written expressly for him.

Immersed in its teachings, Omni felt a profound shift. The world around him seemed to recede as a vision unfurled in his mind's eye, a vast, radiant wheel turning within him, its spokes glimmering with colors he had no words for. He felt the stirrings of something ancient and eternal awakening within his soul.

That night, Omni left the bookstore with the book clenched tightly to his chest, his mind alight with questions and possibilities. The world seemed different now, alive with mystery. And for the first time in years, the emptiness within him felt as though it might one day be filled.

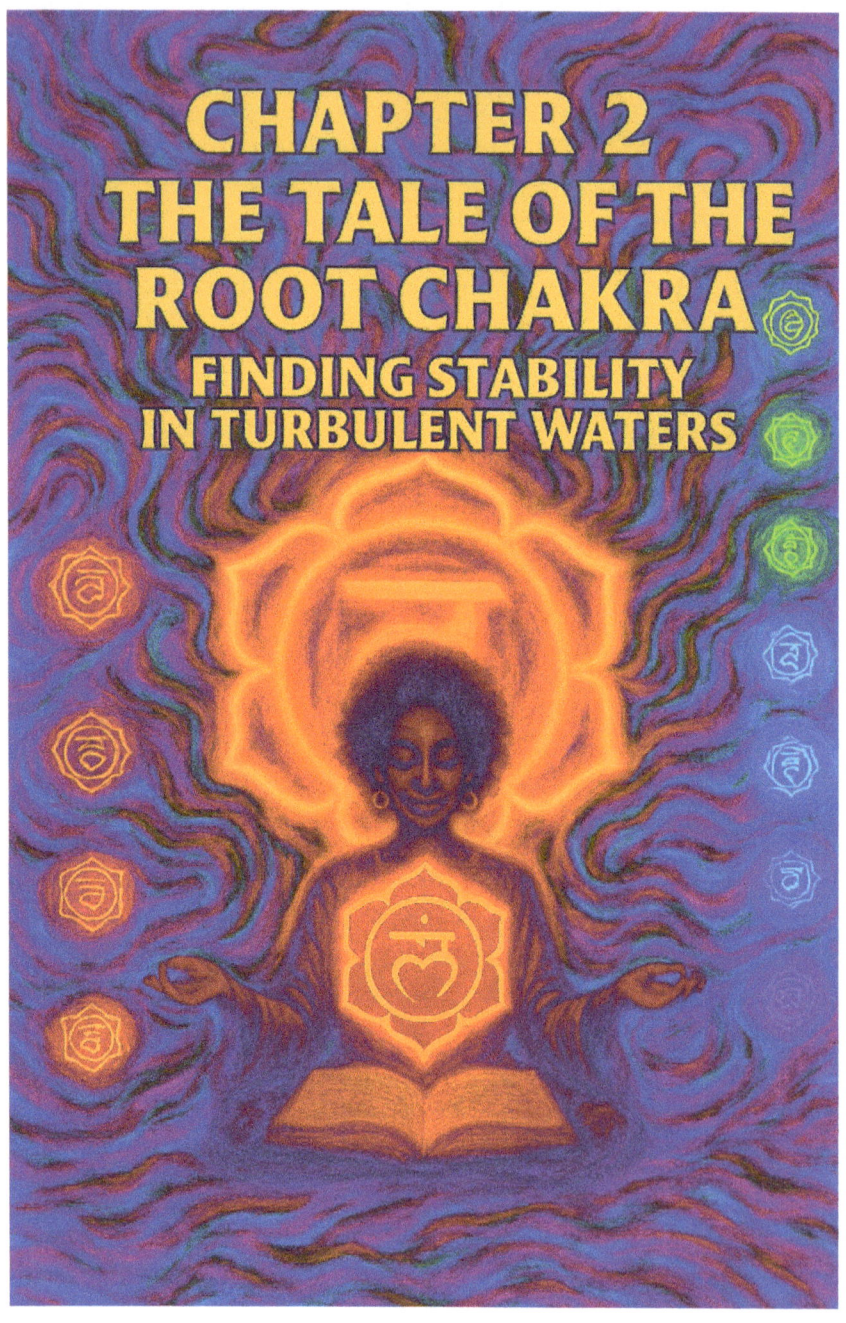

CHAPTER 2: THE TALE OF THE ROOT CHAKRA

Finding Stability in Turbulent Waters

The morning was crisp and golden, the kind of autumn day that seemed painted by the hand of a benevolent god. Omni found himself standing at the edge of a dense forest, its canopy ablaze with amber and scarlet leaves. The scent of damp earth and fallen foliage filled the air, grounding him in the moment.

The book, the one he had discovered the night before in the quiet bookstore, was tucked firmly under his arm. He had spent hours poring over its pages, absorbing its wisdom like a man starved for truth. Each chapter seemed to unlock something dormant within him, whispering secrets that felt both foreign and deeply familiar.

As he turned the page, a peculiar sensation washed over him. The words seemed to ripple, their letters shifting and glowing softly before his eyes. A wave of dizziness overtook him, and when he blinked, the world had changed.

He was no longer in the same forest. Instead, he stood in what seemed like a magical forest out of a movie, his breath forming faint clouds in the cool air. The book was still in his hands, but its pages had grown blank, as if waiting for a new lesson to unfold.

A rustling ahead drew his attention. As he rounded a bend in the path, his breath caught in his throat. Before him stood a figure, an old man clothed in robes of saffron and gold, their colors shimmering as though imbued with sunlight.

The Sage exuded an aura of serene wisdom. His face, lined with age, radiated a kindness that seemed to touch the very air around him. His eyes, dark and luminous, held the weight of centuries yet sparkled with childlike wonder. He stood beneath an ancient oak tree whose gnarled branches stretched like arms toward the heavens.

"Welcome, seeker," the Sage said, his voice rich and melodious. It was a sound that seemed to echo not just in Omni's ears but in his very soul. "I have been waiting for you."

Omni's grip on the book tightened. "This book led me here," he said, his voice barely above a whisper, "It spoke of chakras, of ancient wisdom. And now, I am... here."

The sage's smile deepened, "You are exactly where you are meant to be." He gestured for Omni to sit beneath the oak tree. As Omni settled onto the soft grass, the Sage began to speak, his words carrying the cadence of an ancient song.

"The chakras," he said, "are like the roots and branches of a great tree. They anchor us to the earth and stretch toward the heavens, connecting us to the infinite. The root chakra, the first and most vital, is the foundation. Without it, the tree cannot stand."

Omni turned the book's pages, and as if in synchrony, words began to appear, mirroring the sage's lesson. The text pulsed with a quiet energy, reinforcing the wisdom he was receiving.

The Sage closed his eyes, his voice dropping to a reverent whisper, "Let me tell you a story."

He spoke of a seed planted in barren soil, a seed that held within it all the potential of the world. Over centuries, it faced storms, droughts, and upheavals, its fragile roots struggling to hold fast. But the seed persevered, drawing strength from the depths of the earth. In time, it grew into a mighty tree, unshaken by even the fiercest storms.

"This," the Sage said, "is the lesson of the root chakra. To stand tall in the face of life's tempests, you must ground yourself in the present, draw strength from your inner truth, and trust in the stability of your own being."

As the sage's words settled over him, Omni felt a shift deep within. He closed his eyes and envisioned roots extending from his body into the earth, anchoring him. A profound sense of peace washed over him, a calm he had never known.

When he opened his eyes, he was somehow back in his apartment, the morning sun streaming through the windows. The book rested in his lap, the page he had last read glowing faintly before settling into stillness.

He exhaled a slow, steady breath. This was only the beginning.

CHAPTER 3: AWAKENING THE SACRAL CHAKRA

Navigating the Waters of Creativity and Emotion

The morning air was thick with the scent of blooming jasmine, mingling with the earthy aroma of damp soil. Omni found himself in a garden unlike any he had ever seen before. It seemed to stretch endlessly, a living tapestry of vibrant colors and gentle sounds. Butterflies flitted among clusters of lavender and marigold, their wings catching the dappled sunlight that filtered through the canopy of towering trees. Somewhere nearby, a brook babbled softly, its melody harmonizing with the distant trill of birdsong.

The book was still in his hands, its pages no longer blank but filled with new words that seemed to glow faintly in the soft light. It had guided him here, just as it had before, unfolding its teachings as he progressed on his journey.

At the center of the garden sat the sage, cross-legged on a moss-covered stone. His saffron robes glowed faintly in the morning light as though they, too, were part of this magical realm. Omni approached with reverence, his heart stirring with anticipation for what lay ahead.

"Come, young seeker," the Sage said, his voice a soothing balm to Omni's restless thoughts, "Sit with me, and let us dive deeper into the mysteries of the self."

Omni settled onto the grass, the cool blades brushing against his palms. The Sage regarded him with a quiet smile before closing his eyes as if attuning himself to the rhythms of the world around him. When he spoke, his voice carried the cadence of a gentle river, flowing effortlessly.

"The sacral chakra, Svadhisthana, is the sacred center of creativity and emotion," the Sage began, "It resides just below the navel, where the waters of life swirl and flow. To awaken it is to unlock the wellspring of your passions, your joys, and your ability to create."

Omni turned the page, and as if in harmony, the words of the Sage appeared in the book. He closed his eyes and focused on his breath. The sage's words seemed to guide him inward, drawing his awareness to the ebb and flow of energy within his body.

"Feel the waters within you," the Sage continued, his voice low and melodic. "They are the tides of your existence, the currents of your creativity and emotion."

As Omni embraced this awareness, the book in his hands shimmered once more, revealing the next chapter of his unfolding journey.

The sage's voice softened as he prepared to tell a tale, "Let me share a story, one that reflects the essence of the sacral chakra."

He spoke of a gifted sculptor named Arin, who lived in a distant land. Arin possessed an unparalleled ability to carve beauty from stone, his hands breathing life into the inanimate. His sculptures told stories, captured emotions, and inspired all who beheld them. Yet despite his gifts, Arin struggled. He was tormented by self-doubt, haunted by the fear that his work would never be enough. He sealed his emotions away, believing that vulnerability would weaken him.

One day, a wandering musician visited Arin's village. She played a haunting melody that stirred the hearts of all who listened. She saw Arin's sculptures and knew his heart carried the same depth of expression. "Why do you not carve what you feel?" she asked.

"I do not trust my emotions," Arin admitted, "They are unpredictable, like the tides. I fear they will drown me."

The musician smiled, "But emotions are not meant to be controlled. They are like a river when you let them flow, they nourish the land. When you dam them, they stagnate."

That night, Arin dreamed of a river coursing through a valley, its waters carrying both joy and sorrow. When he awoke, he took up his chisel with a new understanding. He sculpted not with his mind but with his heart. His work became raw, filled with passion, and more beautiful than ever before.

The sage's voice carried the lesson to Omni. "The sacral chakra teaches us that emotions are a source of power, not weakness. Creativity flows when we allow ourselves to feel, express, and release. To embrace this chakra is to embrace the dance of life."

Omni opened his eyes, his heart brimming with newfound understanding. The sage's words resonated deeply, like an echo reverberating through the chambers of his soul. He thought of his own emotions the joy he often suppressed, the sorrow he feared to confront, and saw them not as obstacles but as the waters that could nourish his soul.

"Thank you," Omni said, his voice trembling with gratitude, "Your wisdom has illuminated a part of me I didn't know existed."

The Sage smiled, his eyes twinkling, "This is only the beginning, young seeker. The sacral chakra is a gateway. Beyond it lies the fire of the solar plexus, the heart's boundless love, the voice's truth, and the vision of the third eye. Your journey will take you to all these places, but for now, let the waters of the sacral chakra carry you forward."

Omni rose to his feet, feeling as though the garden itself had imbued him with its vitality. The air seemed brighter, the sounds sharper, and the colors more vivid. He bowed deeply to the Sage before turning to leave, his steps lighter than they had been in years.

As the book pulsed once more, its golden light surrounded him, dissolving the garden into streaks of shimmering energy. When the light faded, he was back in his own space, the book resting in his lap, its pages filled with the lesson he had just lived.

He exhaled slowly, running his fingers over the cover. The story of Arin lingered in his mind, a reminder that life's waters were not to be feared but embraced. The sacral chakra had awakened within him and, with it, the promise of a life lived in the fullness of creativity, emotion, and joy.

CHAPTER 4: THE ODYSSEY OF THE SOLAR PLEXUS CHAKRA

Empowering Self-Confidence and Willpower

The book pulsed in Omni's hands, its golden glow radiating warmth against his skin. As he turned the page, the world around him shimmered and blurred. The familiar room dissolved, replaced by a vast, open landscape. The transition was seamless, as though the book had transported him not only through knowledge but through reality itself.

Omni found himself standing at the edge of a great chasm not a physical one, but an internal abyss that threatened to swallow him whole. Doubt clung to him like a shadow, whispering insidious tales of inadequacy and failure. It reminded him of every mistake he had ever made, every opportunity he had let slip away. The weight of it was crushing, and for the first time since he had begun his quest, he felt his resolve falter.

He turned the book over in his hands. Its pages shimmered, guiding him toward the sacred forest he had visited before. The golden sunlight filtering through the trees cast long, dappled shadows, yet the beauty of the scene did little to soothe his troubled mind. He arrived before the sage, his shoulders slumped, his gaze fixed on the ground.

The Sage sat cross-legged beneath an ancient cedar, his posture as steady and unyielding as the tree itself. He watched silently as Omni approached, his weathered face radiating calm. When Omni finally began to speak, his voice trembled with vulnerability. He poured out his fears, each word tinged with the weight of his struggles. "I feel like I'm not enough," he confessed, his voice breaking. "I don't know if I have the strength to continue."

The Sage listened without interruption, his eyes soft with understanding. When Omni fell silent, the Sage reached out, placing a hand gently on his shoulder. "You are not alone in this," he said. "Even the strongest among us face such doubts. But these moments of uncertainty are not the end they are the crucible in which true strength is forged."

Omni looked up, his eyes searching the sage's face for answers. The old man smiled and gestured for him to sit. "Let me tell you a story," the Sage said. "It is a tale of courage, determination, and the power that lies within the Solar Plexus Chakrathe seat of your willpower and self-confidence."

The book pulsed in Omni's lap as the sage's voice grew rich and melodic, drawing him into another world the words lifted from the page, weaving a tapestry of images before his eyes.

"In a land of rolling hills and verdant valleys," the Sage began, "there lived a warrior named Kai. He was not the mightiest of his people nor the swiftest, but he was known for his unshakable spirit. Where others wavered, Kai stood firm, driven by an inner fire that refused to be extinguished."

Omni felt himself pulled into the story. He saw Kai, a figure clad in simple armor, his eyes fierce with determination, as he stood at the edge of a dark forest. The trees loomed ominously, their twisted branches clawing at the sky like skeletal fingers. Somewhere within the forest lay a dragon, a creature of shadow and flame that terrorized the land. Many had tried to defeat it, but all had failed.

"Kai knew the dangers," the Sage continued. "But he also knew that the dragon's reign of terror could not continue. Armed with little more than his courage and an unshakable belief in his purpose, he stepped into the forest."

Omni could almost feel the chill of the forest air, hear the crunch of leaves beneath Kai's boots, and smell the acrid scent of ash that lingered in the dragon's wake. The path was treacherous, winding through dense undergrowth and over jagged rocks. Yet with each step, Kai drew upon the power of his Solar Plexus Chakra, the fiery center of his being that radiated strength and resolve.

"Doubt whispered to him as it whispers to us all," the Sage said. "But Kai silenced it with action. He reminded himself of his purpose, of the lives depending on him. Each time the fear crept in, he reignited the fire within, letting its warmth drive him forward."

After days of relentless pursuit, Kai reached the dragon's lair, a cavern that yawned like the maw of some great beast. The air was thick with heat and the flicker of molten light. And there, in the heart of the cavern, the dragon awaited. Its scales gleamed like polished obsidian, and its eyes burned with an intelligence as old as the earth itself.

Omni's heart raced as the Sage described the battle that followed. Kai fought not only with his blade but also with his spirit. Each clash of steel against scale sent shockwaves through the cavern, yet Kai did not falter. He drew deeper and deeper into the wellspring of his Solar Plexus Chakra, channeling its boundless energy to fuel his every strike. The dragon roared, unleashing torrents of flame, but Kai stood firm, his inner fire burning brighter than the beast's fury.

"In the end," the Sage said, his voice swelling with triumph, "Kai delivered a final, decisive blow, one born not of brute force but of unwavering belief in his own strength. The dragon fell, its shadowy form dissipating into nothingness. And as Kai stood victorious, he felt a profound sense of clarity. He had not merely defeated the dragon but conquered the doubts and fears within himself."

Omni opened his eyes as the book pulsed once more, signaling the lesson's completion. He felt the weight of his own doubts begin to lift, replaced by a warmth that radiated from his core. "The Solar Plexus Chakra," the Sage said gently, "is your inner sun. It burns with the power to illuminate even your darkest fears. When you trust in its light, you will find the strength to overcome anything."

The Sage rose to his feet, his robes swaying in the gentle breeze. "The dragon you face is no different from Kai's," he said, his gaze piercing. "But you, too, have the power to prevail."

As the golden light of the book engulfed him, Omni felt the forest dissolve around him. The energy of the lesson coursed through his veins, anchoring the wisdom within him. When the light faded, he was back in his own world, the book resting gently in his lap.

The warmth within his chest remained. The path ahead was still uncertain, but Omni no longer feared the challenges it held. For within him blazed the light of the Solar Plexus Chakra, a beacon that would guide him forward, no matter the obstacles.

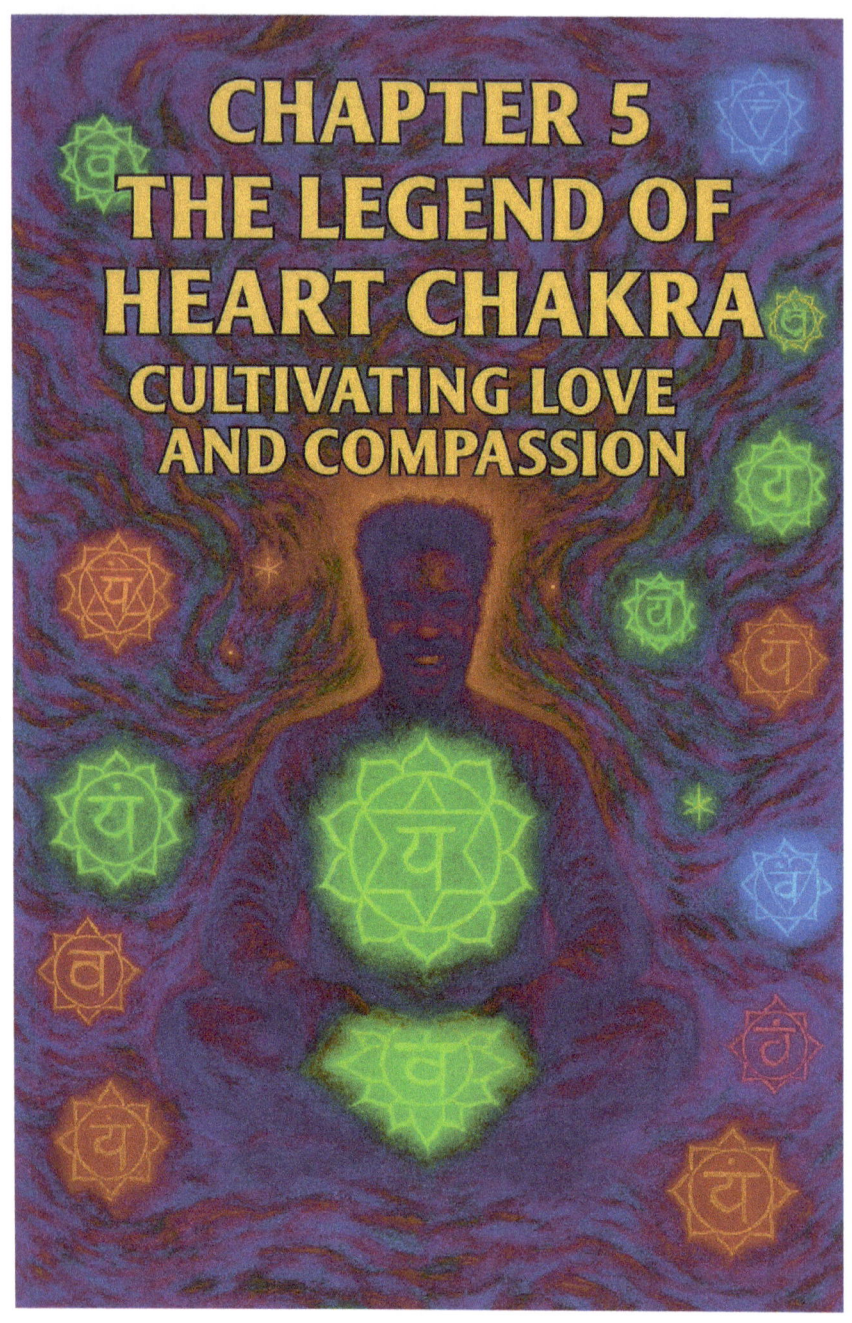

CHAPTER 5: THE LEGEND OF THE HEART CHAKRA

Cultivating Love and Compassion

The book lay open before Omni, its pages alive with shifting words that pulsed like a heartbeat. A warmth emanated from its spine, spreading through his fingertips as if urging him onward. He inhaled deeply, sensing the familiar transition beginning, his surroundings blurred, the air hummed with an unseen force, and the fabric of reality dissolved around him like mist in the morning sun.

When the world reshaped itself, he found himself standing at the edge of a breathtaking valley. The air here was thick with the scent of wildflowers, a fragrant symphony of lavender, chamomile, and rose. The golden light of the sun bathed the land in serenity, casting a warm glow over rolling fields and the crystalline stream that wound its way through the valley's heart.

Omni took a hesitant step forward, his pulse steady despite the wonder that surrounded him. He knew the book had led him here, just as it had before, guiding him deeper into its wisdom. The stream's gentle murmur beckoned him forward, and as he followed its course, he soon spotted the sage.

The old man sat cross-legged on a blanket of moss, his presence as natural as the wind moving through the trees. His eyes were closed, his face serene, yet as Omni approached, the Sage spoke without opening his eyes.

"Welcome, young seeker," he said, his voice carrying the weight of lifetimes. "I see you have come with a yearning in your heart. Tell me, what brings you here?"

Omni lowered himself onto the grass, feeling the earth beneath him. He traced his fingers over the book's cover, gathering his thoughts before speaking. "I feel... disconnected," he admitted. "From others, from myself. It's as if something in me is closed off, preventing me from truly embracing life."

The Sage nodded knowingly. "You speak of the Heart Chakra," he said, his voice gentle. "Anahata, the center of love, compassion, and unity. When it is blocked, we become isolated, trapped within walls of fear and resentment. But when it is open, we are able to love freely, forgive deeply, and connect with the boundless spirit of the universe."

Omni leaned forward, eager for the wisdom the Sage had to offer. The book in his hands grew warmer, its pages shifting slightly as if readying to record the knowledge he was about to receive. The old man's gaze softened as he began to speak.

"Let me tell you a story," the Sage said. "A tale of love and forgiveness that holds the key to unlocking the mysteries of the Heart Chakra."

The sage's voice wove a vivid tapestry, drawing Omni into the world of the story. "Long ago," he began, "in a lush and verdant valley much like this one, there lived a humble farmer named Kobi. He was a man of simple means but extraordinary kindness, tending his fields with care and nurturing the land that sustained him. To those who knew him, Kobi was a beacon of love, a man who gave freely and asked for nothing in return."

Omni closed his eyes, imagining the farmer's life. He saw Kobi rising at dawn, his hands calloused but gentle as he worked the soil. He heard the laughter of children as Kobi shared the fruits of his labor with the village, his heart swelling with joy at their gratitude.

"But Kobi's life was not without hardship," the Sage continued. "For years, he harbored resentment toward his neighbor, a wealthy merchant named Hiro. Hiro coveted Kobi's land and had made several attempts to buy it, each time with thinly veiled disdain for Kobi's simple life. Though Kobi refused to sell, the bitterness lingered between them, festering like a wound."

Omni felt a pang of recognition. How often had he held onto grudges, allowing them to fester? He leaned in closer, eager to hear what came next.

"One year," the Sage said, "disaster struck. A great storm ravaged the valley, and Hiro's crops were destroyed. The merchant, once so proud and self-assured, was brought to the brink of ruin. His family went hungry, and his once-booming trade ground to a halt."

Omni could see it clearly, the once-grand merchant's home was now silent and somber, its windows dark. Hiro, his pride shattered, stared hopelessly at the barren fields.

"And then," the Sage said, his voice softening, "something remarkable happened. Kobi, despite his grievances, gathered the best of his harvest and brought it to Hiro's door. He knocked and waited, his arms full of grain and fruit."

Omni felt a lump rise in his throat as the Sage continued. "At first, Hiro was too proud to accept. 'Why would you help me?' he demanded, his voice sharp with anger. 'I have done nothing to deserve your kindness.' But Kobi simply smiled and said, 'Because love is greater than pride, and compassion is stronger than resentment.'"

The Sage paused, letting the weight of the words settle. "In that moment," he said, "something shifted within Hiro. His anger and pride melted away, replaced by a deep and abiding gratitude. With tears in his eyes, he accepted Kobi's gift. Over time, the two became not just neighbors, but friends, their bond forged in the fires of forgiveness and compassion."

Omni opened his eyes, the tale lingering in his heart. The book in his lap shimmered, absorbing the sage's wisdom into its pages.

"The Heart Chakra," the Sage said, "teaches us that love is the greatest force in the universe. It allows us to see beyond our own pain and anger, to connect with others on a level that transcends all boundaries."

The Sage gestured to the valley around them. "Look at the flowers, young seeker. Each one is unique, yet together, they create something beautiful. So too must we learn to embrace both our differences and our shared humanity."

Omni sat in silence, the beauty of the valley mirrored in the peace blooming within him. He felt a shift deep in his chest, a softening as though a door had been opened. The tale of Kobi and Hiro resonated in his soul, a reminder that love and forgiveness had the power to heal even the deepest wounds.

The book in his hands pulsed, and the valley around him shimmered. The air grew lighter, the colors brighter, as the world around him began to dissolve. In an instant, he was back where he had started, the book now still upon his lap, its pages filled with the story he had just lived.

Omni exhaled slowly, his heart full. He ran his fingers over the book's cover, knowing it had brought him yet another lesson. The sage's words echoed in his mind, love is greater than pride, and compassion is stronger than resentment. As he closed the book, he carried its warmth within him, ready to embrace the next chapter of his journey.

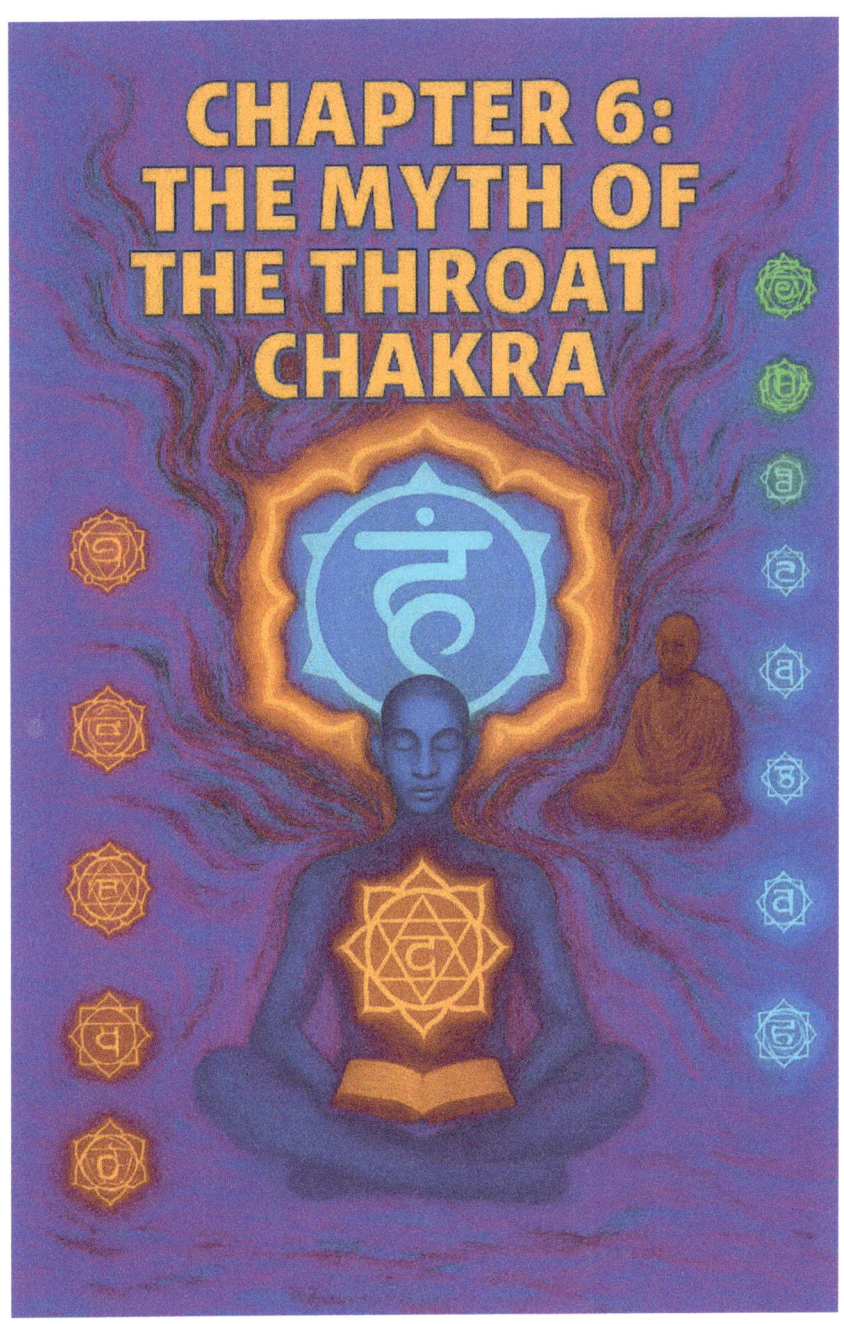

CHAPTER 6: THE MYTH OF THE THROAT CHAKRA

Speaking Truth and Authenticity

A whisper of wind stirred the pages of the book before Omni could even touch it. The words glowed faintly as though waiting for him to proceed. He hesitated. Something about this moment felt different more personal, more urgent. A sensation bloomed in his chest, rising into his throat, tight and unspoken.

The air around him wavered, shifting like ripples across a still pond. He closed his eyes. When he opened them again, the world had changed.

He stood in a lush garden, where the scent of blooming jasmine mingled with freshly turned earth. The leaves above whispered as a gentle breeze passed through, and ahead of him, seated in quiet meditation, was the sage.

Omni's fingers curled around the book's edges as he took a hesitant step forward. He had made great progress, yet something still weighed upon him, a silence, a barrier he could not break through. Words lingered within him, unspoken and uncertain, tangled in doubt. He approached the sage, seeking the wisdom he knew would be waiting.

The old man opened his eyes slowly, as if he had been expecting Omni's arrival. His saffron robes swayed slightly with the breeze, and his gaze held the serenity of one who had long since mastered the art of silence and speech alike.

"Welcome, young seeker," the Sage said, his voice as calm as the flowing stream that meandered through the garden. "I see the words within you, struggling to be freed."

Omni lowered his head. "I want to speak my truth," he admitted, his voice barely above a whisper. "But the words... they don't come. And when they do, they feel weak, like they don't matter."

The Sage nodded, his expression gentle. "You speak of the Throat Chakra, Vishuddha," he said. "It is the bridge between your inner world and the outer one, the voice that carries your soul's truth into existence. When it is blocked, your voice falters, and your truth remains hidden."

Omni's grip on the book tightened. "How do I find my voice?" he asked.

The Sage smiled knowingly. "Let me tell you a story."

His voice shifted, taking on a melodic quality, pulling Omni into the tale. "Long ago, in a land of towering mountains and endless skies, there lived a man named Ashoka. Ashoka was known throughout the land for his wisdom, his words carrying the weight of the heavens. But there was a time when he, too, had been voiceless."

Omni closed his eyes, picturing the scene. He saw Ashoka as a young man, hesitant, his lips pressed shut as he held his thoughts inside, fearing rejection, doubting his worth.

"One day," the Sage continued, "Ashoka met a hermit who lived by a river. The hermit sensed the turmoil within him and said, 'Speak, young one. Let the river hear your truth.' But Ashoka shook his head and whispered, 'I have nothing to say that matters.'"

Omni felt a pang of recognition. How often had he dismissed his own voice as unworthy?

"The hermit smiled and gestured to the river. 'Do you see how it flows?' he asked. 'It does not question its path, nor does it hold back for fear of where it might go. It simply moves, allowing itself to be shaped by the earth yet remaining true to its essence.'"

The sage's voice softened. "Inspired by the hermit's words, Ashoka began to speak, not to impress, not to be accepted, but simply to express what lay within him. He spoke to the wind, to the trees, to the stars above. With each word, he felt lighter, more free. And in time, his voice grew strong, carrying his truth far and wide."

Omni let out a slow breath, the weight in his throat loosening. "So, to open the Throat Chakra," he said, "I must speak without fear? Without seeking approval?"

The Sage nodded. "Speak with honesty, with sincerity. Let your words reflect the truth within you, and they will carry their own power."

The book in Omni's hands warmed, its pages shifting slightly, absorbing the wisdom imparted. The Sage gestured toward the nearby stream. "Go," he instructed. "Speak to the water. Let it carry your voice."

Omni hesitated, then stepped forward. He closed his eyes and let the words come, at first quiet, uncertain, but then stronger, bolder. He spoke of his doubts, his dreams, his fears, and his hopes. The stream carried his words away, their echoes joining the melody of the flowing water.

When he turned back to the sage, his heart felt lighter, his voice steadier. The old man smiled. "You have taken the first step," he said. "Your Throat Chakra is open now, a conduit for your truth. Nurture it, and it will never fail you."

As the garden around him shimmered, the book pulsed once more, pulling him back. The scents, the sounds, the light all faded, and when he opened his eyes, he was seated once more with the book upon his lap, its pages filled with the lesson he had just lived.

Omni traced the words on the page, feeling their weight, their truth. He had found his voice. And with it, the strength to speak his truth, no matter where his journey led him next.

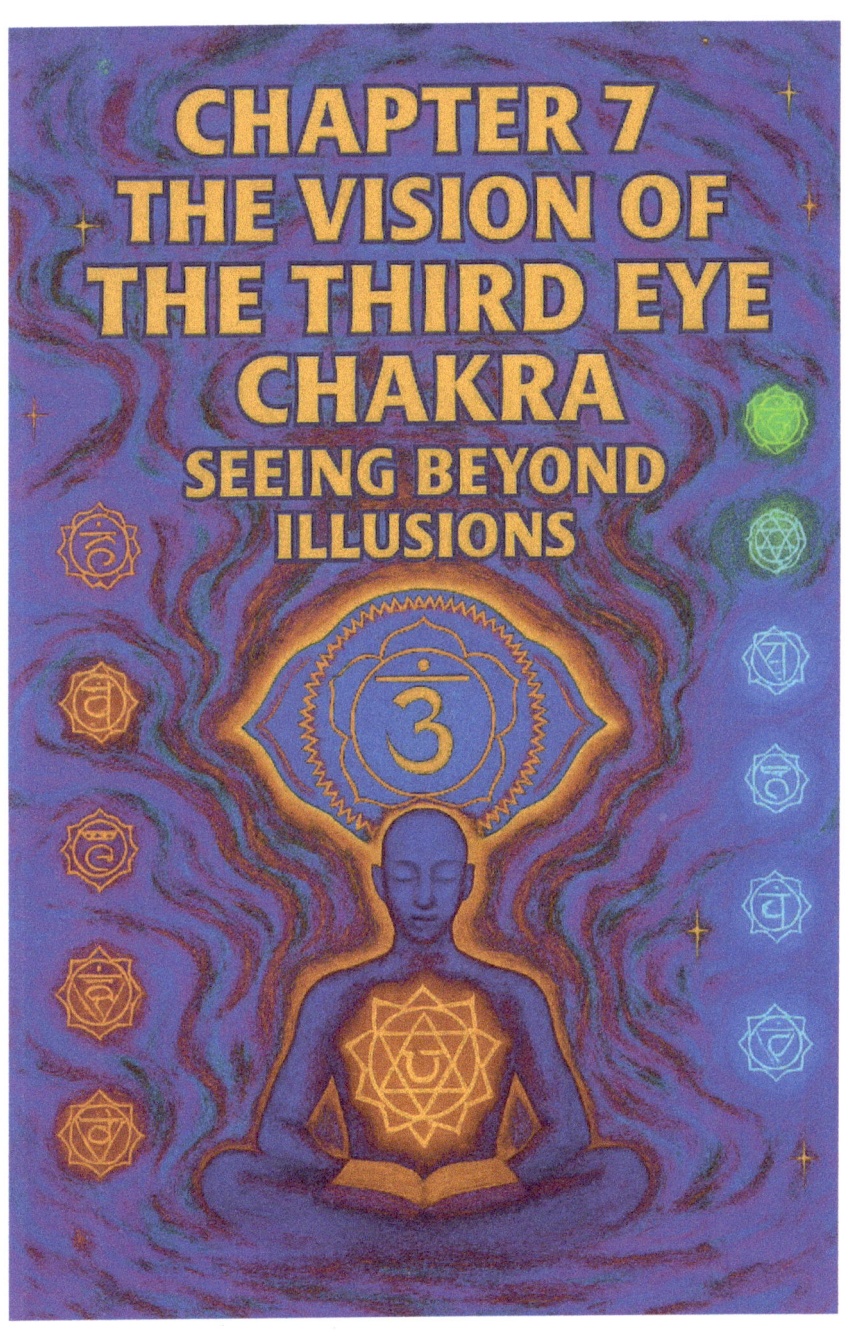

CHAPTER 7: THE VISION OF THE THIRD EYE CHAKRA

Seeing Beyond Illusions

The book lay open before Omni, but this time, it did not glow or pulse with energy. Instead, its pages remained still as if waiting for him to be ready. He ran his fingers over the worn edges, feeling a subtle shift in the air. A sensation, not a pull, but an invitation settled over him. Unlike before, this transition was not abrupt. It was slow and intentional. A veil lifting.

His surroundings faded, dissolving into streaks of indigo and silver. When the world reassembled, he found himself standing on a high plateau, the ground beneath him solid yet untamed. Jagged cliffs framed the landscape, and below, a valley stretched endlessly, its depths hidden beneath swirling mist. The sky above stretched vast and infinite, speckled with the first stars of twilight.

A presence stirred behind him. Omni turned to find the Sage standing at the plateau's edge, gazing into the mist below. His saffron robes billowed slightly in the wind, yet he remained as still as the stone beneath his feet.

"This is the place of sight," the Sage said, his voice carrying on the wind. "Where the eyes of the body can no longer see, the eye of the soul begins to open."

Omni stepped forward, his heart already quickening with anticipation. "You speak of the Third Eye Chakra," he said. "The gateway to intuition, to seeing beyond illusion."

The Sage nodded, motioning for Omni to sit beside him on a smooth, flat stone. "Ajna," he said, speaking the chakra's name with reverence. "It resides between the brows, the seat of inner perception. To open it is to see the world as it truly is, not as your mind tells you, but as it exists in infinite complexity."

Omni hesitated, his thoughts tangling like threads. "But how can I see without my eyes?" he asked. "How can I trust what I cannot touch or measure?"

The sage's lips curled into a knowing smile. "The physical senses show you only a fraction of reality. They are limited by perception, by conditioning, by the walls you have built within your mind. The Third Eye is the key to dissolving these illusions."

Omni listened intently as the Sage continued. "Let me tell you a story," he said, settling deeper into his seat. "A story of the weaver and the web."

The sage's voice deepened, painting the tale in the air around them. "Long ago, in a land of towering mountains and endless skies, there lived a woman named Asha. She was a weaver of unparalleled skill, her hands crafting intricate patterns into cloths of silk and gold. People came from far and wide to see her work, marveling at its beauty."

Omni closed his eyes and saw her in his mind, a woman seated at a loom, fingers dancing over threads that gleamed in the candlelight.

"One day," the Sage continued, "a traveler arrived at Asha's workshop. He was an old man with eyes like storm clouds, and he carried with him a riddle. 'Weaver,' he said, 'your patterns are magnificent, but do you see the design beneath them all?'"

Asha frowned. "What do you mean?" she asked. "The patterns I create are right before me."

The old man chuckled. "Close your eyes, and I will show you."

Intrigued, Asha obeyed. And in the darkness behind her lids, she began to see something extraordinary, a web of light, vast and infinite, stretching across the universe. Each thread pulsed with energy, connecting stars to rivers, mountains to hearts, dreams to reality. She realized then that her loom was but an echo of this cosmic web, her work a reflection of the greater pattern that bound all things together.

"When Asha opened her eyes again," the Sage said, "she saw the world differently. She no longer wove merely for beauty; she wove to honor the unseen connections she had glimpsed. Her work became a reflection of a truth that could not be captured by sight alone."

The Sage fell silent, allowing the story to settle over Omni like a mist rolling in from the valley. "The Third Eye," the Sage said at last, "is your window to this greater web. It allows you to perceive the patterns that bind all things together, to see beyond the veil of illusion."

Omni felt a stirring within him, a faint awareness, like a thread just beyond his grasp. "How do I open it?" he asked. "How do I see what Asha saw?"

The Sage closed his eyes and breathed deeply, his presence radiating calm. "Begin by stilling the mind," he said. "The Third Eye cannot open while the waters of thought are turbulent. Breathe, young seeker. Let go of the need to understand and simply be."

Omni followed his guidance, inhaling deeply. The cool air filled his lungs, then left in a slow, steady exhalation. With each breath, the chatter of his mind quieted, the edges of his awareness softening.

"Now," the Sage murmured, "bring your focus to the space between your brows. Imagine a light there, a small, steady flame, glowing softly in the darkness."

Omni did as he was told, and a faint light began to form in his mind's eye. It flickered at first, fragile and hesitant, but with each breath, it grew steadier, brighter. As the light expanded, he felt his perception shift. The mist around him dissolved, and in its place, the web appeared, a lattice of shimmering light stretching into infinity. Every action, every thought, sent ripples through the web. It was breathtaking, humbling, and overwhelming all at once.

When Omni opened his eyes, tears streaked his face, though he could not say why. The Sage smiled knowingly. "You have glimpsed the truth," he said. "The Third Eye is open. Trust it, and it will guide you."

The book pulsed in Omni's lap, its warmth wrapping around him. The plateau, the mist, the sage, all faded as the familiar hum of the book's energy grew stronger, pulling him back. When he opened his eyes again, he was seated once more, the book resting gently in his hands, its pages filled with the lesson he had just lived.

Omni exhaled, his heart brimming with awe. He had seen beyond the veil. And with this newfound sight, he knew his journey was far from over, there was still more to learn, more to perceive. As he traced his fingers over the glowing pages, he whispered a silent vow: to trust in the vision granted to him and to walk forward with eyes truly open.

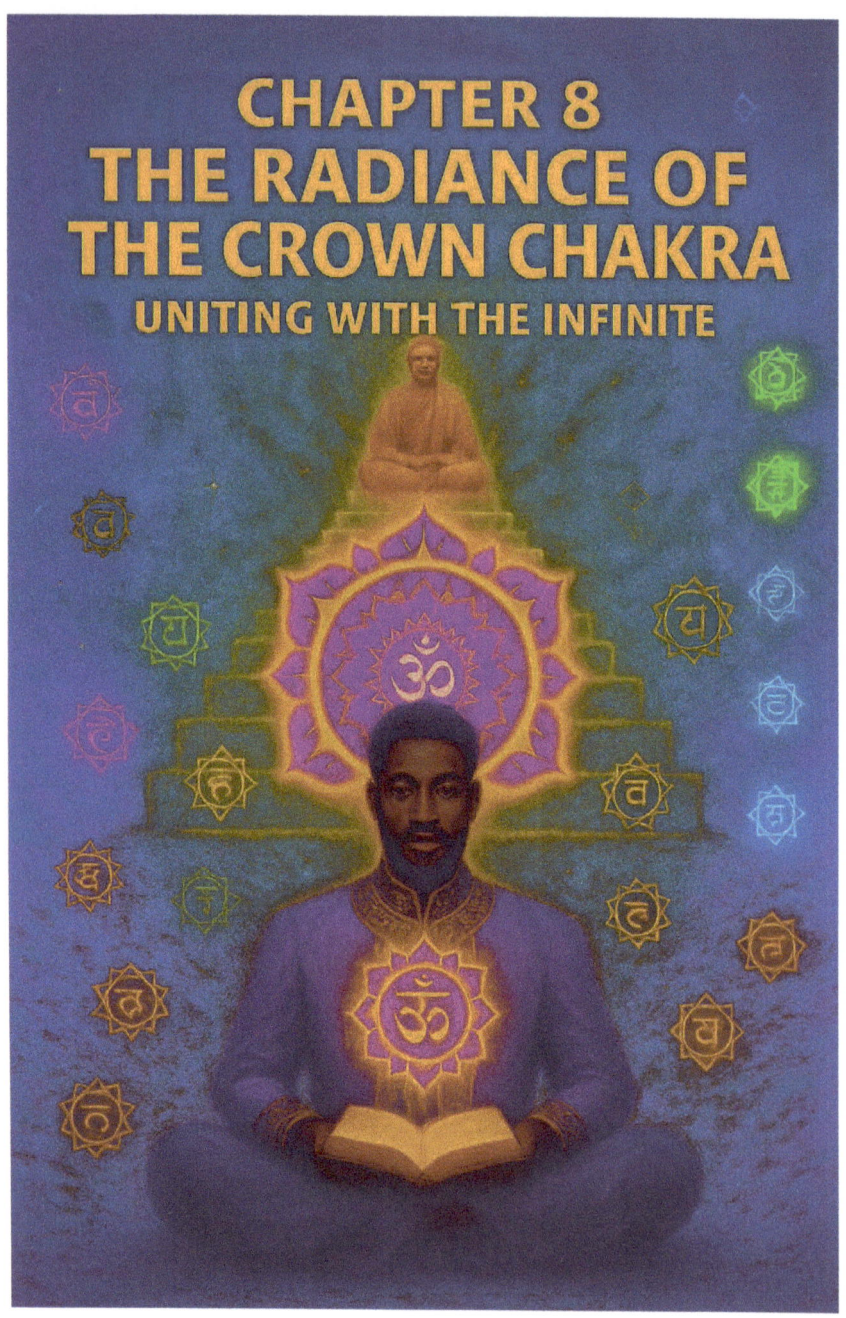

CHAPTER 8: THE RADIANCE OF THE CROWN CHAKRA

Uniting with the Infinite

A strange stillness settled over Omni as he traced his fingers over the book's worn cover. Unlike before, there was no hum, no pulse of energy guiding him forward. Instead, the pages before him remained blank, an expanse of untouched possibility. He inhaled deeply, sensing that this final lesson would be different. Not a pull, but a release. Not a journey outward but a return to something he had always known.

As he exhaled, the edges of the world softened, dissolving like mist in the morning sun. The weight of the physical faded, and he found himself standing at the base of an endless sky. A spiraling path stretched before him, carved not of earth but of light. With each step, the sky grew brighter, shifting from deep violet to a luminous gold. The air shimmered with a quiet hum, the very essence of existence vibrating all around him.

At the path's peak, the Sage sat upon an unseen throne, his presence both solid and ethereal. His form pulsed like starlight as if he existed beyond the confines of any single place. Omni approached, a sense of weightlessness overtaking him. He was no longer just walking, he was ascending.

"You have come far, young seeker," the Sage said, his voice carrying the resonance of something eternal. "The final chakra lies before you—Sahasrara, the Crown Chakra. It is the gateway to the infinite, the seat of divine consciousness."

Omni knelt before him, a deep knowing stirring within. "I feel as though I've climbed mountains within and without," he said. "But I don't yet understand. What does it mean to unite with the infinite?"

The sage's eyes glowed softly like the light of dawn breaking over a still ocean. "To unite with the infinite is to dissolve the illusion of separation," he said. "The Crown Chakra is the thousand-petaled lotus, unfolding into boundless light. It is where you remember that you are not apart from the universe, you are the universe."

Omni felt something within him shift, a quiet unraveling of every barrier he had ever built. "How do I reach it?" he asked.

The Sage gestured for him to sit, and together, they faced the endless sky. "The journey to Sahasrara is not one of effort but of surrender," the Sage said. "You do not climb to it; you dissolve into it. Let me tell you a story."

His voice was softer now, carrying not just words but the echoes of something eternal. "In a time before time, there was a drop of water resting in the palm of the ocean. The drop longed to know itself, to understand its place in the vastness of the sea. It traveled far and wide, seeking answers in the waves, the tides, the currents."

Omni saw it in his mind's eye—a single, glistening drop, shimmering with reflected light.

"But no matter how far it traveled, the drop felt incomplete," the Sage continued. "It asked the waves, the winds, the sun, 'Who am I?' But none could answer. Finally, weary from its search, the drop surrendered. It let go of its striving and allowed itself to merge with the ocean."

The sage's eyes met Omni's, steady and profound. "And at that moment, the drop realized the truth: it was never separate from the ocean. It had always been the ocean, a part of its infinite wholeness."

Omni felt a shiver run through him. "You are the drop," the Sage said. "And the universe is the ocean. Sahasrara is the moment when you let go of the illusion of separateness and remember your oneness with all that is."

The Sage rose and gestured toward the glowing horizon. "Come," he said, "There is something you must experience."

He led Omni to the very edge of the sky itself, where the world seemed to dissolve into pure light. "Close your eyes," the Sage instructed, "Focus on the crown of your head. Imagine a lotus there, its petals tightly closed. With each breath, let it open."

Omni obeyed, his awareness narrowing to the top of his head. He envisioned the lotus, a radiant flower, its petals shimmering with golden light. With each breath, it unfurled, layer by layer, until it was fully open.

"Now," the Sage continued, "feel the light of the universe pouring into the lotus. Let it flow through you, dissolving every boundary, every thought, every sense of self."

At first, Omni felt only the steady rhythm of his breath. But then, slowly, a warmth began to build—a gentle, luminous sensation spreading from the crown of his head to the depths of his being. It was as though he were bathed in pure light, each cell vibrating with divine energy.

And then, it happened.

The boundaries of his existence vanished. The sense of self, of individuality, dissolved like mist in the morning sun. He felt himself expanding outward, becoming the wind, the sky, the infinite cosmos itself. He was not just a part of the universe, he was the universe. There was no separation, no division. There was only light, only presence, only the eternal hum of existence.

In this state, there was no fear, no longing, no striving. There was only peace, an all-encompassing stillness that resonated with the very core of creation. Omni felt tears flowing, though they were no longer his. They belonged to the ocean, flowing through the drop.

When he opened his eyes, the world around him shined with a newfound clarity. The sky was more radiant, the air more alive. But more than that, Omni himself had changed. The emptiness that had once haunted him was gone, replaced by an unshakable knowing, he was whole, he was infinite, he was one with all things.

The Sage watched him with a serene smile. "You have touched the infinite," he said, "This is the gift of the Crown Chakra. It is not something you achieve but something you remember. Carry this light with you, young seeker, and let it guide you."

The book pulsed in Omni's lap, its warmth enveloping him like a gentle embrace. The sky, the sage, the path, all faded as the familiar hum of the book's energy drew him back. When he opened his eyes, he was seated once more, the book glowing softly in his hands, its pages filled with the lesson he had just lived.

Omni exhaled, his heart radiant with peace. He traced his fingers over the sacred pages, knowing that he had reached the final step of his journey. But the journey itself was infinite, unfolding in every breath, in every moment. As he closed the book, he whispered a vow, not an ending, but a beginning.

To live as a drop in the ocean. To embrace the vastness within. To walk forward, not as a seeker, but as one who had finally seen.

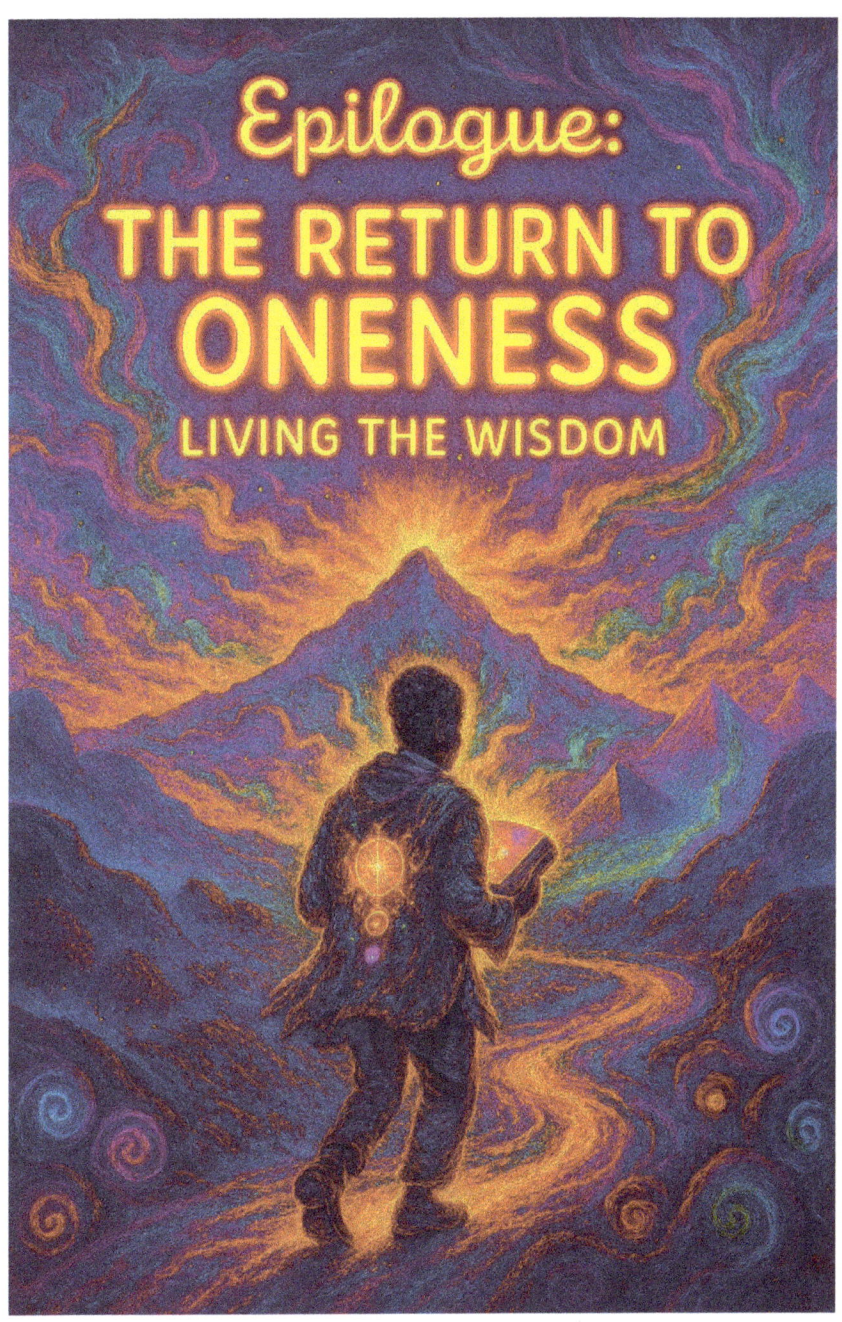

EPILOGUE: THE RETURN TO ONENESS

Living the Wisdom

The book pulsed softly in Omni's hands, its familiar warmth radiating through his fingers. As he turned the final page, the golden light within it expanded, wrapping around him like a gentle embrace. The world shimmered, and when the light receded, he found himself descending the mountain, his journey complete.

The first light of dawn crept over the horizon, painting the sky in hues of amber and rose. The air was crisp, filled with the scent of dew-kissed earth, and every step he took felt purposeful. It was as though the mountain itself were bidding him farewell, whispering its silent wisdom in the rustling wind. He turned to look back at the peak, now shrouded in mist and golden light. It seemed distant yet near as if existing beyond time itself.

With a deep breath, Omni continued forward, carrying the light of his awakening with him, knowing that the journey did not end here, it had only just begun.

Returning to the World

The city welcomed him with its usual symphony of life. The rhythm of hurried steps, the honking of horns, the chatter of voices—it was all the same, yet different. Where once the noise had seemed overwhelming, now it was a melody, a dance of energy and movement. Everything was interconnected, and Omni could feel the pulse of life flowing effortlessly around him.

As he walked, he passed a group of children playing, their laughter ringing through the air like chimes in the wind. A stray ball rolled toward him, and he picked it up, tossing it back with a smile. "Thanks, mister!" one of the children beamed.

Omni watched them for a moment, marveling at the purity of their joy. It was a reminder that the universe spoke in the simplest moments, in the laughter of children, in the song of the wind, in the hush of the world settling into dusk.

Further along, he came across a street musician playing a haunting melody on a violin. The music carried the weight of longing and hope, a silent story woven into the notes. Omni closed his eyes, allowing the melody to wash over him, feeling the depth of its emotion.

He reached into his pockext and placed a folded bill into the musician's open case. Their eyes met, and the man nodded in silent gratitude. "Thank you," he murmured.

Omni smiled. "Thank you for sharing your gift."

In every face he passed, he saw something deeper, a reflection of the divine, a story waiting to be heard. There was no separation, only connection, only oneness.

Sharing the Light

Word of Omni's transformation spread quietly but unmistakably. Friends, colleagues, and even strangers sensed something different about him, an unshakable peace that seemed to radiate from within.

One evening, his friend Maya invited him for tea, her small apartment filled with the scent of chamomile and the warmth of books lining the walls. She studied him over the rim of her cup, curiosity flickering in her eyes. "You're different," she said. "It's like you're carrying something... luminous."

Omni chuckled. "Luminous? That's a generous word."

"I mean it," Maya insisted. "You seem... lighter. Freer. What happened?"

Omni sipped his tea, searching for the right words. "I went on a journey," he said finally. "Not just across mountains and valleys, but within myself. I learned to see the world, and myself—with new eyes."

Maya listened intently as he shared his experiences, from the grounding of the root chakra to the vast transcendence of the crown. He did not speak as a teacher but as a companion, his words simple, honest, and open.

"You make it sound so attainable," Maya murmured. "Like this isn't some distant thing but something we all have inside us."

"Because it is," Omni said gently. "The light you see in me is the same light that exists in you. It's just waiting for you to uncover it."

Maya exhaled, her gaze thoughtful. "I think I'd like to start my own journey."

Omni smiled. "I'll be here if you ever need guidance. But remember, the path is yours to walk."

And so, in quiet moments like these, seeds of curiosity and awakening were planted in those around him. He did not preach, nor did he seek to change others, he simply lived his truth and, in doing so, became a light for those who wished to see their own.

Zen'in Sh*t

THE ENDLESS JOURNEY

One evening, as the sun dipped toward the horizon, Omni wandered to the river's edge at the outskirts of the city. The water flowed quietly, reflecting the masterpiece of oranges and purples painted across the sky. He stood in stillness, letting the peace of the moment wash over him.

He closed his eyes, inhaling deeply, feeling the cool air fill his lungs. In the silence, he sensed the movement of the universe, the gentle rhythm of the river, the rustling of the leaves, the distant call of birds. He was not separate from these things; he was a part of them, and they were a part of him.

A memory surfaced, his time on the mountain when he had glimpsed the infinite web of existence. The drop and the ocean are inseparable and eternal. He felt it again now, that profound sense of unity, as though the boundaries of his being had dissolved entirely.

Tears welled in his eyes, though they were not tears of sadness or joy. They were tears of recognition, of knowing. He had sought enlightenment, yet enlightenment had been with him all along, waiting for him to remember.

As he turned to leave, the last rays of the sun dipped below the horizon, the world shifting into twilight. Street lamps flickered to life, casting their warm glow on the path ahead. Omni walked forward, his heart light, his spirit open.

The journey was not over, it never truly would be. The path of wisdom, of connection, of unity, was not a destination but an eternal unfolding. And as he moved through the city, through life, through each breath and moment, the light within him burned bright, illuminating every step he took into the infinite.

AFTERWORDS: A GRATEFUL ACKNOWLEDGMENT

In closing, this journey of self-discovery and enlightenment, I am filled with deep gratitude and appreciation for all who have supported and inspired me along the way. Among those who have played a pivotal role in the creation of this book, there is one individual whose influence and guidance have been particularly profound, my dear brother Kam.

Kam, you are a true brother, a kindred spirit whose presence in my life has been a source of infinite love, respect, and inspiration. From the moment we met in Peru, our connection was undeniable, and I knew that our paths were destined to intertwine in ways that would forever change the course of my journey. It was you, Kam, who planted the seed of inspiration into the creation of: **Zen'in Sh*t: Journey to Chakra Mastery.**

Through our shared experiences and heartfelt conversations, I am filled with a profound sense of gratitude for the transformative impact you have had on my life. Your presence has been a gift beyond measure. So, to you, my dear brother Kam, I offer my deepest thanks and appreciation for your unwavering support, your divine vibes, and your infinite wisdom.

With love and gratitude,

Ra'El

ABOUT THE AUTHOR

Mystic. Oracle. Storyweaver of the Eternal.

Ra'El OmniZen is not merely an author, he is a portal. A bridge between dimensions. A divine mirror reflecting your own infinite potential back to you.

From a childhood of constant movement, 13 schools, countless shelters, cities, and states to match. Ra'El was tempered by impermanence and awakened through experience. By 16, he could speak in glossolalia (tongues), and had already tasted the raw edge of leadership. By 18, he was forged in discipline, becoming one of the elite few chosen for the U.S. Air Force Honor Guard. There, he rose to become the Head Trainer of the Drill Team, mastering form, rhythm, and presence on a global stage.

But true mastery would come later.

After leaving the military, Ra'El answered a higher calling, one that spoke not through systems, but through spirit. In the jungles of Colombia, Peru, and Mexico, guided by sacred plant medicines, he died to the illusion of self and was reborn in remembrance. Speaking in tongues. Channeling light codes. Merging with lion spirits and dragon consciousness. Witnessing the Tree of Life. Receiving visions of past, future, and Source in a single breath.

He did not choose the name Ra'El OmniZen.
It was given to him.

Ra'El – The Divine Sun of the Most High

OmniZen – The All, expressed through stillness and eternal Nirvana

He is the founder of OmniZen, a global spiritual movement rooted in Zealous Eternal Nirvana—a path where ancient wisdom, cosmic law, African ancestral memory, and raw modern truth converge. His work lives at the intersection of mysticism, mindfulness, and multidimensional mastery.

His books are not just words on a page.

They are transmissions—each one encoded with frequencies to awaken your inner truth.

They don't just inform.

They initiate.

Whether he's guiding sacred ceremonies, teaching the next generation of spiritual warriors, or channeling divine messages through poetic parables, Ra'El speaks not to your mind, but to your remembrance.

You didn't find this page by accident.

Your soul brought you here.

You're not just reading about him.

You're remembering you!

www.ingramcontent.com/pod-product-compliance
Lightning Source LLC
LaVergne TN
LVHW061627070526
838199LV00070B/6609